Who Says Women Can't Be COMPUTER PROGRAMMERS?

The Story of Ada Lovelace

Tanya Lee Stone

Illustrated by Marjorie Priceman

Christy Ottaviano Books
Henry Holt and Company
New York

Henry Holt and Company, *Publishers since 1866*
Henry Holt® is a registered trademark of Macmillan Publishing Group, LLC
175 Fifth Avenue, New York, NY 10010
mackids.com

Library of Congress Cataloging-in-Publication Data
Names: Stone, Tanya Lee, author. | Priceman, Marjorie, illustrator.
Title: Who says women can't be computer programmers? : the story of Ada Lovelace /
Tanya Lee Stone ; illustrated by Marjorie Priceman.
Description: First edition. | New York : Christy Ottaviano Books : Henry Holt and Company, [2018]
Audience: Ages 5–8. | Includes bibliographical references.
Identifiers: LCCN 2016050390 | ISBN 9781627792998 (hardcover)
Subjects: LCSH: Lovelace, Ada King, Countess of, 1815–1852—Juvenile literature. |
Women mathematicians—Great Britain—Biography—Juvenile literature. | Mathematicians—
Great Britain—Biography—Juvenile literature. | Computers—History—19th century.
Classification: LCC QA29.L72 S76 2017 | DDC 510.92 [B]—dc23
LC record available at https://lccn.loc.gov/2016050390

Our books may be purchased in bulk for promotional, educational, or business use.
Please contact your local bookseller or the Macmillan Corporate and Premium Sales Department
at (800) 221-7945 ext. 5442 or by e-mail at MacmillanSpecialMarkets@macmillan.com.

First edition, 2018 / Designed by Liz Dresner
The artist used gouache and india ink on hot-press watercolor paper to create the illustrations for this book.
Printed in China by RR Donnelley Asia Printing Solutions Ltd., Dongguan City, Guangdong Province

1 3 5 7 9 10 8 6 4 2

For everyone who thinks outside the box

—T. L. S.

On the outskirts of a lovely village in County Kent, England, down a long driveway lined with lime trees, lived a young girl with a wild and wonderful imagination. As Ada was often left alone, she grew quite good at entertaining herself with interesting ideas.

Ada's cat, whom she named Madame Puff, was an attentive audience. Unlike Ada's mother, Madame Puff never issued her the reward of a paper ticket when she did well—and never took the ticket away when she was thought to be bad. And Madame Puff never, ever made her stand in a dark closet until she promised to behave.

Ada's mother, Lady Byron, wasn't trying to be mean. In her own way, she was hoping to protect her daughter, protect her from what Lady Byron believed were the dangers of a vivid imagination such as her father had.

Ada's father was Lord Byron, a world-famous poet who was almost as famous for his bad behavior as he was for his poetry. Before Ada's parents had been married a year, Lady Byron got so fed up with him, she wrapped her baby girl in a warm blanket and moved back into her parents' house. Ada was only five weeks old.

A few months later, owing enormous sums of money, Lord Byron leaped into a gilded coach he hadn't paid for, raced to the coast, scrambled onto a ship setting out for France, and fled England. He never saw his daughter again.

Lady Byron decided the best way to make sure Ada didn't grow up to have a wild imagination like her father was to train her to think like a mathematician, so she hired tutors for Ada from the time she was four.

By the time she was eight, Ada's nimble mind was soaking up music, French, and math more than six hours a day. Despite all the studying and the unfortunate fact that she was often ill, the fiery Ada was interested in lots of other things, too—drawing, writing, singing, and playing the piano and violin.

When Ada was twelve, she became consumed with the idea of designing a flying machine in the shape of a horse and crafting wings for herself, modeling them after bird wings. But instead of giving Ada the bird-drawing books she asked for, Lady Byron increased Ada's hours of math studies.

Lady Byron was also determined to tame her feisty daughter and make sure Ada married a suitable man. In the early 1800s, it was extremely difficult—even for a well-educated woman like Lady Byron—to picture anything more for a daughter than to become a proper lady and wife.

When Ada was almost eighteen, Lady Byron presented her to the royal court. Ada enjoyed curtsying to King William and Queen Adelaide in her white satin and tulle gown. But it was a different kind of gathering they attended that Ada found much more intriguing.

Mary Somerville

Charles Dickens

Charles Babbage

A fascinating scientist named Charles Babbage liked to surround himself with interesting people. He had a reputation for throwing loud parties at his house. People would crowd in for the lively conversation— and to see what new contraption Babbage might show off next!

By 1833, there were already basic calculators that could do simple problems, such as . . .

$$2 + 3 = 5$$

$$100 + 300 = 400$$

But Charles Babbage had invented a machine he called the Difference Engine, which could do automatic calculations up to twenty or even thirty numbers long, such as . . .

$$1,769,462 - 348,250 = 1,421,212$$

On the night Ada met Charles, he talked about his machine "as a child does of its plaything." Twelve days later they met again, so Charles could demonstrate the model he had built. Ada was enchanted by the beauty she saw in his invention.

...and of course numbers! Geometry, algebra...
...mechanical equations of an almost...
it is mathematics that is Poetical!

possibilities for calculating ...infinite ...enchantress of numbers... numerical patterns & not only numbers & equations unknown Quantities

This was a major turning point for Ada. She was excited to realize that math and imagination did not have to be opposites—as her mother had wanted so desperately to impress upon her—they actually went together! Ada saw in Charles a person with whom she could discuss ideas. A great friendship started to grow. Dozens of letters went back and forth between them, and they would visit each other, likely walking and talking math and philosophy.

As for the Difference Engine, building the entire thing turned out to be too expensive. But Charles's mind was already racing toward an even better idea—a new machine that could do *any* kind of math calculation based on instructions it was given. He called it the Analytical Engine.

Charles had seen a weaving loom called the Jacquard loom, which used cards with specially placed holes punched in them. Each card told the loom what color thread or design to weave next. The Jacquard loom was able to weave complicated patterns in cloth. Some of the designs even looked like paintings! Perhaps most important, there was no limit to what the punch cards could instruct the loom to do.

Charles knew he could adapt this punch-card system to give his math machine unlimited instructions. This was something entirely new in the world of calculations. His engine was also capable of doing things Charles himself did not yet comprehend.

But Ada did.

She was familiar with how the Jacquard loom worked, and she understood mathematics. Those things—combined with what she called "the fair white wings of imagination"—made it possible for Ada to see "the unseen worlds around us." She understood that the engine would be able to weave numbers.

And, as she later wrote, "Just as the Jacquard-loom weaves flowers and leaves, it can do whatever we know how to order it to perform."

Ada was the perfect person to help Charles get some much-needed attention and money for his invention so he could afford to actually build it. When Charles went to Europe to talk about his engine, he and another mathematician wrote a paper about it, but it was in French. This was Ada's opportunity to help. She translated the paper into English and showed it to Charles.

His reaction surprised her: "I asked why she had not herself written an original paper. . . . I then suggested that she should add some notes."

As smart and sassy as Ada was, that idea had never crossed her mind. In the 1800s, women simply didn't do things like write scientific papers. But, of course, she set right to it!

$$\triangle \, nu_z = C:$$

$$12) \, \Sigma \, (n+2)(13...23),(24...25),$$

$$u_z = a + bX + CX + ...MXn-1$$

Throughout this time Ada was often ill. She pressed on anyway, with a passion for the project that turned up in many of her letters to Charles. "No more for tonight, for I can neither talk, write, nor think. . . . And yet I feel more like a fairy than ever."

When she was done, her notes were twice as long as Charles's original paper, and her notes became much more famous. For Ada had envisioned—and then described—what Charles hadn't realized: his Analytical Engine not only had the power to process numbers, but it would be able to create things like pictures and music—just as computers do today!

Charles never raised the money he needed for his invention, but if the Analytical Engine had been built at the time, it is quite possible that the entire age of computers would have begun more than one hundred years earlier than it did. And in large part we would have Ada, with her brain of a mathematician and her imagination of a poet, to thank.

More to the Story

There are always fascinating details I'm not able to work in when I'm writing a nonfiction picture book. Sometimes it's excruciating to leave certain details out—like the grand European tour Lady Byron took Ada on when she was ten; or how Ada spent nearly three years in bed between the ages of thirteen and fifteen, combating what was probably polio and suffering partial paralysis; or how Charles Babbage went to great lengths to acquire a fabric portrait of Joseph-Marie Jacquard, inventor of the Jacquard loom, to display in his house. Collaborating with Marjorie Priceman is such a wonderful adventure because I'm able to share ideas with her as she makes her own decisions about the visual layers she will add to the story. For example, after seeing that some of her sketches incorporated numbers and words, I was inspired to find real equations for her to use.

Lord Byron is a subject who could fill several books, but my focus here was Ada's contribution to the future of the computer. Still, it bears mentioning that as decadent and flawed as Lord Byron was, especially as a father, he did love his daughter and felt tortured by their separation (though he did nothing to change it). During that tumultuous crossing of the English Channel when he fled England for France, he wrote the first three stanzas of the third canto of *Childe Harold's Pilgrimage*, which included these lines: "Is thy face like thy mother's, my fair child! / Ada! sole daughter of my house and heart? / When last I saw thy young blue eyes they smiled, / And then we parted. . . ."

Ada's parents, however estranged, seem to have independently come to the same conclusion that Ada should not end up like her father. Before he died, Byron said, "I hope the Gods have made her anything save poetical—it is enough to have one such fool in the family."

Hardly a fool, the brilliant Ada had a lot going on. In the decade between the time Charles first thought of the Analytical Engine and Ada published her notes about it, she also married William King in 1835 and had three children within four years. Ada was most certainly the dominant figure in the household, with William happy to let her take charge. He was quite aware that she was smarter than he, and it didn't seem to bother him. She, however, did grow tired of his lack of ambition. She craved a partner who was her intellectual equal and wanted to do great things. Fortunately, she found that in her friendship with Charles. The combination of those two relationships seems to have brought her happiness, and Charles was a frequent visitor to the family's home.

There is much more to learn about Ada. There were joys and adventures as well as times of financial hardship. Sadly, she died from what is believed to have been uterine cancer just before her thirty-seventh birthday.

Charles also has a fascinating history. His massive soirees certainly provided Ada with the intellectual company she so craved. Guests included celebrities of the time such as Charles Darwin, Charles Dickens, Florence Nightingale, Mary Somerville, and Alfred Lord Tennyson. As for Charles Babbage's Difference Engine, a working model was built in the 1990s using his original designs. It is on permanent display at the Science Museum in London, England. Charles was still perfecting his designs for the Analytical Engine at the time of his death at age seventy-nine. The work both Ada and Charles accomplished laid a foundation for scientists to draw upon in the future.

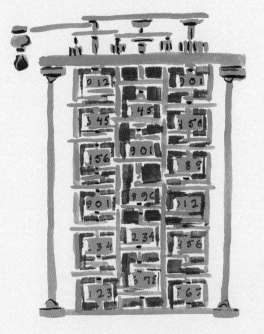

About Ada's Name

If you learn more about Ada, you will discover that she is often referred to by different names—Ada Byron, Ada Lovelace, the Countess. Her given name at birth was Augusta Ada Gordon, as she was the daughter of George Gordon. He was commonly referred to as Lord Byron, and she went by her middle name, Ada, so she was commonly called Ada Byron.

When she married William King, her formal name became Augusta Ada King. When William became the Earl of Lovelace, she became Augusta Ada King, Countess of Lovelace—or simply Lady Lovelace. The name Ada Lovelace is not at all accurate, yet it seems to have stuck!

Sources

Essinger, James. *Ada's Algorithm: How Lord Byron's Daughter Ada Lovelace Launched the Digital Age*. Brooklyn, NY: Melville House, 2014.

Isaacson, Walter. *The Innovators*. New York: Simon & Schuster, 2014.

Krysa, Joasia. *Ada Lovelace, Introduction: 100 Notes—100 Thoughts*. Berlin: Hatje Cantz, 2011.

Toole, Betty Alexandra. *Ada, the Enchantress of Numbers: Prophet of the Computer Age*. Mill Valley, CA: Strawberry Press, 1998.

Woolley, Benjamin. *The Bride of Science: Romance, Reason, and Byron's Daughter*. New York: McGraw-Hill, 1999.

Quotations

"as a child does of its plaything": Essinger, p. 81.

"the fair white wings of imagination" and "the unseen worlds around us": Toole, p. 94.

"just as the Jacquard-loom weaves flowers and leaves": Essinger, p. 169.

"it can do whatever we know how to order it to perform": Krysa, p. 120.

"I asked why she had not herself written an original paper. . . . I then suggested that she should add some notes.": Essinger, p. 150.

"No more for tonight, for I can neither talk, write, nor think. . . . And yet I feel more like a fairy than ever": Toole, p. 153.

"I hope the Gods have made her anything save poetical—it is enough to have one such fool in the family": Essinger, p. 55.